3/2014

soulmate!

SPIRITUAL TIDBITS
for
EVERYDAY LIVING

Love

Madeline

SPIRITUAL TIDBITS
for
EVERYDAY LIVING

REVEREND MADELINE

authorHOUSE®

AuthorHouse™ LLC
1663 Liberty Drive
Bloomington, IN 47403
www.authorhouse.com
Phone: 1-800-839-8640

Published by AuthorHouse   03/10/2014

ISBN: 978-1-4918-4893-7 (sc)
ISBN: 978-1-4918-4892-0 (e)

Library of Congress Control Number: 2014900171

Any people depicted in stock imagery provided by Thinkstock are models,
and such images are being used for illustrative purposes only.
Certain stock imagery © Thinkstock.

This book is printed on acid-free paper.

In Appreciation

~~~~~~~~

In much gratitude to all the spiritual seekers who
have traveled before us, making our path clear.

Thanks to Creator, family and friends for
all the love and support in the creation of
this little book. Special thanks for all the
heroes on the 12 Step paths of recovery.

~~~~~~~~

Dedication

~~~~~~~

Dedicated to my earth angels:
My Beloved Yolanda
My Family
Ms. Theresa Morrison
Ms. Vi Strandberg
Ms. Alice O'Brien
And
Mr. Theodore Chen

Thank you for touching my heart and
enhancing my relationship with God.

~~~~~~~

Note to the Reader

~~~~~~~~

Within these pages you will find spiritual terms: God, Jesus, Creator, Meher Baba, Higher Power, Great Spirit, etc . . . We ask you to substitute our words for those that work for you. We believe this method will allow all readers to benefit from the true essence of each message.

There is a Spiritual Tool Kit of fifteen action items that can help you develop or enhance your spiritual growth. Each has been numbered, yet there is no need to do them in order. They are proven methods that help us connect with our fellow humans and God; especially, in times of turmoil or when feeling alone and isolated.

If you find something inspiring, enlightening or magical, please share it with someone you think could benefit. Be well on your journey, my friend.

~~~~~~~~

~~~~~~~

May this new day bring forth love
and light at your every turn!

~~~~~~~

~~~~~~~

Life is short.
Don't take a moment
for granted, trust the journey, pray
for others and love full heartedly!

~~~~~~~

~~~~~~~~

You are a beautiful child of God!

~~~~~~~~

~~~~~~~~

The way we treat each other is a
direct reflection of how we treat ourselves.
Be good to yourself!

~~~~~~~~

~~~~~~~

Spiritual Tool #1
Make a gratitude list.

Daily write down any 5 things that you are grateful for in your life. Learn how to cultivate your gratitude.

Here are some examples:

Day 1	Day 2
Jesus	Sobriety
Recovery	Sunset
Washed car	Dating
Family	Siblings
Pets	iPod

~~~~~~~

~~~~~~~~

Today, take the risk to extend your heart;
you may be surprised at the outcome!

~~~~~~~~

~~~~~~~~

Don't take life too seriously.
Laugh at yourself every once in a while.
Make time to play and be silly
Your body and soul will appreciate it.

~~~~~~~~

~~~~~~~

If you worry, pray.
If you pray, don't worry.

~~~~~~~

~~~~~~~

Change is coming. Open your mind
and heart to receive your miracle.

~~~~~~~

~~~~~~~

Spiritual Tool #2
Make a God box.

Create a container that represents your Higher
Power. Keep paper and pen near your God box.
When you need to turn something over to Creator,
write it down and put it in this special container.

This is a physical extension of turning something
over to your God. There isn't anything too big
to go into your God box. As time passes you'll
discover that your God box becomes less problems
and more gratitude, prayers and well wishes.

~~~~~~~

~~~~~~~

Happiness is found in appreciating what
you have, not waiting for what you want.
Cultivate your gratitude and your life will
be a beautiful garden of many riches.

~~~~~~~

~~~~~~~

Find your light and strength within.
Every cell is equipped to move
you forward with purpose.

~~~~~~~

~~~~~~~

Nothing changes if nothing changes.
Doing the same thing over and over,
then expecting different results
can make us crazy.
Pray for the courage and strength to walk
towards the new and different.

~~~~~~~

~~~~~~~

I wouldn't have to LET GO, if I didn't hang on!

~~~~~~~

~~~~~~

Spiritual Tool #3
Create your own spiritual retreat.

For example:
Five days in quiet solitude; minus all electronics:
(iPad, cell phone, computer, laptop,
TV, radio, DVD, CD, etc . . .)
Relax, pray, meditate, exercise and
change your eating habits.
Plug in and connect with God.

~~~~~~~~

~~~~~~~~

Is it my will or God's will?
It's always my will, until I pause and invite God in.

~~~~~~~~

~~~~~~~~

Filling your emptiness with people
or things will not sustain you.
Find your inner Christ and be whole again.

~~~~~~~~

~~~~~~~~

Look someone in the eye, smile and say, "Hi".
You might be the only person they talk to that day.
Extending ourselves is not that difficult
and the affects may be profound.
Many humans live lonely days.

~~~~~~~~

~~~~~~~~

Life is precious, treasure each moment!

~~~~~~~~

~~~~~~~

Spiritual Tool #4
Visit your local Assisted Living Facility.

Ask attending management to
direct you towards someone
who never has any visitors.
Take time to make a new friend.

~~~~~~~

~~~~~~~

Thoughts are things.
How do you think of yourself today?

Do you understand that you have a Universal
essence flowing through you?
This energy is connected to each
and every living thing?
Know you are precious and have purpose.
Seek and you will find.

~~~~~~~

~~~~~~~

The journey is inward.
Stop looking outside of yourself to
seek that which is within.
Let your light shine bright for all to see!

~~~~~~~

~~~~~~

Unfortunately,
"Hurt people, hurt people."

A path of prayer and forgiveness
will lighten your load.
May Creator continue to watch over and guide us all.

~~~~~~

~~~~~~

Making amends, isn't only saying "You are sorry.",
but to change in words and actions.

~~~~~~

~~~~~~~

Spiritual Tool #5

Practice tolerance.

The most loveable quality
anyone can possess is tolerance.

It is the vision that enables one
to see things from another viewpoint.

It is the generosity that concedes to others
the right to their own opinions
and their own peculiarities.

It is the bigness that enables us
to let people be happy in their own way
Instead of our way.

~~~~~~~

~~~~~~~

Children are the closest we can get to God.
Listen to them with your heart and you will be
amazed at their simple and pure wisdom.

~~~~~~~

~~~~~~~

Stop using curse words.
I'm certain you are intelligent and can find
other ways to express your emotions.

~~~~~~~

~~~~~~~

The jailer can't go home until the prisoner
is free. Both are trapped, just opposite sides
of the bars. Let the light warm and heal
your heart, filling it with forgiveness.

~~~~~~~

~~~~~~~

Humility is like ZEN; the moment
you say you have IT,
it's gone.

~~~~~~~

~~~~~~~

Spiritual Tool #6

Donate to your local food bank.

Remember, people have pets that need to eat, too!

~~~~~~~

~~~~~~~

Love is an action word.
Love is best experienced when extended to others.

~~~~~~~

~~~~~~~

What have you co-created with
your Higher Power today?
Be grateful, visualize and believe!
Manifest your reality.

~~~~~~~

~~~~~~~

Walk in the world as a Child of Light.

~~~~~~~

~~~~~~~

If you ever find yourself "unwilling",
pray for the willingness to be willing.

~~~~~~~

~~~~~~~

Spiritual Tool #7

When at a Drive-Thru Fast Food restaurant,
pay for the order behind you.

~~~~~~~

~~~~~~~~

When looking in the mirror, what do you see?

~~~~~~~~

~~~~~~~~

What would your day look like if you
took a vacation from worry?

~~~~~~~~

~~~~~

God is good all the time.
When the waters are murky, He makes pure.
When fog blinds, he lifts, making visible our path.

All the time God is good.

~~~~~~~

~~~~~~~

When we "don't know", that means
there is a lot of room for God.

~~~~~~

Spiritual Tool #8

Grow a vegetable garden.
Take excess food to your local Food Bank.
Everyone will benefit from your riches!

~~~~~~~

~~~~~~~

Honey, we've all made mistakes.
Come on in, have a seat, forgive
yourself and move on.

~~~~~~~

~~~~~~~

Do you know your true purpose?
Seek inward then live forward.

~~~~~~~

~~~~~~~

If you are feelings stagnate with your
practice of prayer and meditation.
STOP.
Go do something else and come back to it later.

~~~~~~~

~~~~~~~

Practice loving Universal Spirit with
your mind, body and soul.
See Her true essence in all things.

When you see a beautiful scenic view or
something that makes your soul smile,
Listen carefully.

God will whisper,
"Do you like it? I made it just for you."

~~~~~~~

~~~~~~~~

Spiritual Tool #9

Pray for others; especially those whom you dislike.
Pray for their well being, happiness & prosperity.
They might not change, yet your attitude
towards them will change.

~~~~~~~~

~~~~~~~~

You are wonderful, simply because you exist.
Let your true purpose shine.

~~~~~~~~

~~~~~~~~
Compassion.
Listening with your heart is one of
the best ways to show respect.

~~~~~~~~

~~~~~~~

Change happens.
Make sure you are spiritually fit
for life's speed bumps.

~~~~~~~~

~~~~~~~

Love yourself as Creator loves you.
We can't give away something we don't have.

~~~~~~~

Spiritual Tool #10

Quick Fix when feeling disconnected from God.
Every time you touch something with your hands say,
"Thank you God."

For example:
Holding keys, pen, cellular phone, coffee cup, etc . . .

Within a short time you will feel joyfully reconnected.

~~~~~~~

~~~~~~~~

Pause, just for a moment and feel the
true essence of God all around & within you.

~~~~~~~~

~~~~~~~~

It's important for us to contribute our time,
energy and love to our fellow humans and God.
Extend yourself and make a positive
difference in your community.

~~~~~~~~

~~~~~~~~

Whatever problem
you are experiencing,
know that your Spiritual Solution is always bigger!

~~~~~~~~

~~~~~~~~

Practice of the spiritual life will
bring peace and serenity
to you and those about you.

~~~~~~~~

~~~~~~~

Spiritual Tool #11

Find one thing today that will provide
hard evidence that there is a power greater
than yourself, working for YOU!

~~~~~~~

~~~~~~~

Learning to respond to life, instead of reacting to it,
requires the use of your PAUSE button.

~~~~~~~

~~~~~~~

The Power of Prayer is a real energy
able to alter an expected outcome.

~~~~~~~

~~~~~~~

Surrender to a Higher Power and
let the winning begin.

~~~~~~~

~~~~~~~

Cultivate your gratitude in all aspects of your life.

~~~~~~~

~~~~~~~

Spiritual Tool #12

Be creative.
Journal, memorize a poem, play an
instrument, paint, etc . . .
Co-create something with your Jesus today!

~~~~~~~

~~~~~~~~

Justified anger?
Have it! Own it!
Just don't be overcome by it, hurt
yourself or someone else.
Simply work through it constructively
as you move towards forgiveness.

~~~~~~~~

~~~~~~~~

Great Spirit doesn't want us to be perfect, but
rather to trust and rely upon Her for all things.

~~~~~~~~

~~~~~~~~

Have a good day, unless you've made other plans.

~~~~~~~~

~~~~~~~~

Learn to appreciate your past; it's
brought you to this very moment!

~~~~~~~~

~~~~~~~~

Spiritual Tool #13

Live today knowing that Love is not
the answer, but the assignment.

Pray for the sick, poor, homeless and hungry,
Then go out and do something about it!
Love is an action word.

~~~~~~~~

~~~~~~~

Highest of the High,
May our hearts be open to Your gifts.
May our inner light shine upon those
who need You the most.
May we learn to entrust all to You
in our heart, mind and body.

~~~~~~~

~~~~~~~

Oh Great Spirit,
Let my heart be open to Your many possibilities.
May Your love shine within and
outward for all those to see.
We welcome Your healing.

~~~~~~~

~~~~~~~

Happy, Joyous and Free!
We are all entitled to the abundance of the Universe.

~~~~~~~

~~~~~~~

With every step you take, know
you are on sacred ground.

~~~~~~~

~~~~~~~

Spiritual Tool #14

Don't let others define who you are
or what you can become!
Unlimited possibilities are your gifts, by God's grace.

~~~~~~~

~~~~~~~~

Within You

Remember that which we call;
Creator, Goddess, Jesus, Universal Spirit, etc . . .
is within you, not outside of yourself.
The true essence lives in each and
every cell. Universal energies flow
through you, just like all things.

Seek within for your courage and strength
during turbulent times. You possess all that you
need to overcome and triumph. Stop thinking
about the problem and turn inward, gathering
faith, strength, courage and solution.
Your spiritual solution is always
bigger than your problem.

~~~~~~~~

~~~~~~~~

You are loved and have great purpose.
BELIEVE.

~~~~~~~~

~~~~~~~

Yes, of course we grieve when we lose a loved one.
Give memory to the good and joyous times.
They were much bigger than the
anniversary of their passing.

~~~~~~

~~~~~~

Use your experiences to help another
get through a rough patch.
Two will be healed.

~~~~~~~

~~~~~~~~

Spiritual Tool #15
Pause, Pray and invite God IN!

~~~~~~~~

Appendix

Reverend Madeline

Reverend Madeline was born, raised and spent a majority of her life in the Pacific Northwest town of Seattle, WA. Currently, she resides on the East Coast in Norfolk, VA. She practices her ministry daily, one heart at a time; offering pastoral care, spiritual guidance and workshops.

Most Sundays, Reverend Madeline prays and celebrates with Living Waters Sanctuary; under spiritual guidance of Pastor Pamela Anne Bro, PhD. Our sacred gathering is open and all inclusive; come join us!

Visit Reverend Madeline at www.peacefulsoul.org
and follow her daily blog.